THE "STOURBRIDGE LION,"
THE FIRST LOCOMOTIVE EVER RUN UPON A RAILROAD IN AMERICA.

Copyright, 1883, by JOHN TORREY.

Steam Locomotives

Whistling, Chugging, Smoking Iron Horses of the Past

by **Karl Zimmermann**
Photography by the author

Boyds Mills Press

for Laurel, Jenn, and Emily

Acknowledgments

The photograph on pp. 22–23 is by Laurel Zimmermann.

My gratitude to the following for providing illustrations from their collections:

William D. Middleton (p. 15)
James D. Porterfield (p. 14)
Jim Shaughnessy (pp. 12, 13, and endpaper image of *Stourbridge Lion*)
Roger Cook (endpaper photo of Roger Cook, on left, with author)

Special thanks to Randal O'Toole of the Pacific Railroad Preservation Association for the use of his rendering of Spokane, Portland & Seattle No. 700 (p. 33).

—K. Z.

Published by Boyds Mills Press, Inc.
A Highlights Company
815 Church Street
Honesdale, Pennsylvania 18431
Printed in China

Publisher Cataloging-in-Publication Data (U.S.)

Zimmermann, Karl.
    Steam locomotives : whistling, chugging, smoking
iron horses of the past / by Karl Zimmermann.—1st ed.
[48] p. : col. ill. , photos. ;   cm.
Includes index.
Summary: An introduction to the history and workings of
steam locomotives.
ISBN 1-59078-165-1
1. Steam locomotives — Juvenile literature.
(1. Locomotives. 2. Railroads — Trains.) I. Title.
625.26/1 21   TJ605.5.Z56 2004
2003111246

First edition, 2004
The text of this book is set in 13-point Minion.
Visit our Web site at www.boydsmillspress.com

10 9 8 7 6 5 4 3 2 1

Contents

Introduction
Love Those Locomotives! 5

One
The Age of Steam Begins 11

Two
From Grasshoppers to Big Boys 17

Three
Bigger and Better 23

Four
How a Steam Locomotive Works 31

Five
The Care and Feeding of the Iron Horses 35

Six
Steam Bows Out .41

Seven
All Aboard for a Ride Behind Steam 45

Author's Note 47

Glossary 47

Index 48

Introduction

Love Those Locomotives!

MANY AN EVENING AS A SMALL BOY, I sat on the sagging wooden steps of my hometown depot and watched as a huge, grimy steam engine pulled in, hauling my father home from New York City, where he worked. I remember seeing the headlight dance into view down the track, shining on the curving rails. The light grew larger and larger, the noise building to a hissing, clanking clamor as the engine swept past me and came to a shuddering halt. I'd spot my dad as he climbed down from the coach. As he hugged me, I'd listen for the steamer to whistle twice, then chug off into the night.

Ever since then I've been fascinated by locomotives, especially those powered by steam.

What was it about steam locomotives that captivated me? Perhaps it was the way they gave up their secrets so willingly, letting me see how they worked. And hear how they worked. And smell. Even feel, for when I stood near a steam locomotive, I was warmed by the blaze in its firebox and the steam in its boiler. I could drink in the aroma of coal smoke and hot grease.

◀ *In South Africa, the* Union Limited, *an excursion train, runs along the Garden Route.*

Best of all was the way the locomotives looked, with lots of moving parts, all clearly displayed. Miracles occur within the lifeless box of a computer, but what is there to see? Steam locomotives were just the opposite, showing all. Tall driving wheels whirred, rods waved frantically, smoke belched from stacks. These machines certainly got my attention — and held it.

Traveling to Photograph Steam

In the summer of 1957, when I was thirteen, my parents gave me a good-quality 35-millimeter camera to replace my box Brownie. I began pointing that camera at the handful of steam locomotives still hauling freight and passengers in the United States. For a few months I didn't need to travel far, since the Pennsylvania Railroad was running the last of its steamers in my home state of New Jersey.

But in October those steamers were retired, gone forever. So my friend Roger Cook and I begged our parents to let us make an overnight rail journey to Roanoke, Virginia. There, on the Norfolk & Western Railway, we would find America's last great steam operation. Hauling coal was the N&W's main business, so the railroad stuck with its coal-burning steam locomotives until management simply had to face the fact that diesels were cheaper to operate. (Roger and I hated these diesels. We saw them as boring, bland intruders vanquishing our beloved steamers.)

We won our point with our parents, so right after Christmas they saw us off aboard a Pullman sleeping car. Our train left New York City's wonderful Pennsylvania Station and headed down Virginia's Shenandoah Valley to Roanoke.

Early morning on the narrow gauge in El Rancho, Guatemala.

In 1957, a Norfolk & Western locomotive leads the Powhatan Arrow *out of Roanoke. The railroad's Tudor-style Hotel Roanoke, where I stayed, is in the background.*

We stayed at the N&W's hotel there, just across the street from the depot. For two days we haunted the station's platforms, watching the railroad's streamliners — modern, lightweight passenger trains — roll through behind huge, sleek, red-and-black steam locomotives.

We visited the railroad's general offices, in a yellow brick building right by the tracks and dusted by locomotive cinders. Ben Bane Dulaney, the N&W's public relations manager, gave us pictures and booklets showcasing the railroad's steam locomotives. Indeed, the Norfolk & Western was still proud of its steamers, among the most modern, most powerful, and most efficient ever built. Mr. Dulaney also arranged for us to tour Shaffers Crossing, the railroad's main switching yard and engine terminal, a three-ring circus of steam. In this smoky scene, trains shunted in all directions, while locomotives were serviced — fed coal and water, greased, and rid of "clinkers" (hard bits of burned-out coal fused together) and old ash that accumulated in their fireboxes. Then they were left on the "ready track," all set once again to haul trains into the Blue Ridge Mountains.

But in two short years all those locomotives were cold, waiting to be scrapped. Their steel would be cannibalized and remade into other products and machines more in demand in the middle of the twentieth century.

In Montreal in 1958, Canadian Pacific No. 2459 is kept gleaming by attentive shopmen.

Off to Canada, Then Around the World

For another few years, steam survived in a few places in Canada, so Roger and I headed north. We recorded scenes of steam in snow, steam chugging down little-used branch lines, steam hauling commuters in and out of Montreal.

During our first visits, the locomotives of the Canadian Pacific gleamed in well-polished black, gray, red, and gold, shining examples of the pride of the railroaders who ran and maintained them. As the months passed, however, the locomotives' boilers dimmed with soot and indifference. Paint cans were put away, along with the polishing rags. In 1960 steam railroading ended in Canada, too.

But there were other places in the world where steam locomotives still worked, and from time to time I would head off to find these survivors. I found steam in Europe, but only briefly. Then in Africa. Eventually in South America.

And, happily, in the United States as well, steam lived on. Even today many locomotives run regularly on "tourist" railroads, some of them operated by volunteer enthusiasts whose goal is to keep the image of the steam locomotive fresh for future generations. Now and again a steam locomotive is even sent out on the "high iron," or main line, to race through the countryside with whistle wailing, trailing clouds of smoke and steam.

On these occasions, countless thousands come to trackside to watch. Like me, they love those locomotives.

It's 1977 in South Africa as a Mountain-type steamer leads a local passenger train.

One

The Age of Steam Begins

BEFORE THE AGE OF STEAM, land travel moved only as fast as a horse could gallop. Overland transportation of goods was limited to what oxen or horses or mules could haul, either over primitive roads or on canals. But the steam locomotive changed all that forever.

In the last years of the twentieth century, computer technology altered the way people live and work. In the late eighteenth and early nineteenth century, the harnessing of the power of steam had done much the same thing. Wood, coal, and later oil were burned to turn water into steam.

Under pressure, that steam could power stationary engines that pumped water or drove machinery. It could send steamboats paddling down inland rivers and around lakes. It could propel ocean liners across the Seven Seas. And it could haul railway trains.

Steam power drove the Industrial Revolution, that era of great social change that began in England in the mid-eighteenth century. What had been a rural nation of farmers became an urban one of factories. And although this movement would bring change to just about every aspect of life in Britain, continental Europe, and North America, nowhere was the change more dramatic than in the way people traveled — and in the ease with which they could ship goods.

◄ *In Ecuador, a narrow-gauge train on the Guayaquil & Quito heads into the mountains. Though it looks small and quaint, the locomotive is hugely more sophisticated than its earliest predecessors.*

Railroading as we know it was born in England, when in 1825 George Stephenson designed the *Locomotion* for the Stockton & Darlington line. It became the first steam engine to serve a public railway. (Even more primitive steam locomotives had been at work in England's coal fields for a number of years.) Typical of the early railways, the Stockton & Darlington was short — only twenty miles long.

Just four years later, in 1829, Stephenson, often called the "Father of Railways," designed a better locomotive, this one for the Liverpool & Manchester Railway. It was called the *Rocket,* which was something of an overstatement since it traveled barely twenty miles per hour.

The First Steam Locomotives in America

Railroad fever spread quickly across the Atlantic Ocean to the United States, a young nation that was fast expanding. The first steam locomotive intended for commercial use in the United States was the *Stourbridge Lion.* In August of 1829, this British-built engine ran in Honesdale, Pennsylvania, on a railroad owned by the Delaware & Hudson Canal Company. This railway was horse-powered and hauled coal from the mines to the canal. Unfortunately, the *Stourbridge Lion* weighed twice as much as its builders had promised. It was far heavier than the flimsy rails could carry, so after its trial runs it was converted to service as a stationary engine.

◀ Left: *Steam railroading began on the Stockton & Darlington with George Stephenson's* Locomotion.

Above: *The first steam locomotive to run in the United States was the Delaware & Hudson Canal Company's* Stourbridge Lion.

The *Stourbridge Lion* looked something like a modern steam locomotive. It had a horizontal boiler with a tall smokestack at the front. The little *Tom Thumb*, which steamed on the Baltimore & Ohio Railroad in Maryland just a few weeks after the *Lion* ran in Pennsylvania, did not. With its vertical boiler, it resembled a coffeepot more than what we tend to think of as a steam locomotive. Similar looking was the *Best Friend of Charleston*, which on January 15, 1831, began service on the South Carolina Railroad. It was the first full-sized steam locomotive to be built in the United States (at

New York's West Point Foundry), and it operated on the country's first commercial steam railway.

The *Best Friend* was quite a success, hauling as many as five cars with fifty passengers. Unfortunately, about five months after its much-praised debut, the locomotive's fireman tied down its safety valve because the hiss of escaping steam annoyed him. When the boiler exploded, he was killed.

In the early years, trains could be a hazardous way to travel. Boiler explosions were common, as were derailments on poorly laid track. Some steps toward safety came with

This replica of the Best Friend of Charleston *reenacts the first run in America of a regularly scheduled steam passenger train.*

the *John Bull*, which first ran on New Jersey's Camden & Amboy Railroad in late 1831. Though the locomotive was built in Britain, it was in the United States that a warning bell and headlight were added. Also added was a pilot or "cow-catcher," which was attached to the front of the engine and designed to push obstructions, including cattle, off the tracks.

Though British builders, particularly George and Robert Stephenson's works, were initially the most renowned, over time America's great locomotive manufacturers would build more than 170,000 locomotives.

The railroad industry had nearly a century of growth ahead when these primitive little locomotives entered service, beginning a radically new era of travel and transport. In time, the little Camden & Amboy would become part of the mighty Pennsylvania Railroad, the self-proclaimed "Standard Railroad of the World." On this railroad and hundreds of others, the steam locomotive would develop and grow in amazing ways.

A Race Between a Horse and an Iron Horse

The Baltimore & Ohio became the nation's first railway when its initial thirteen miles of line opened between Baltimore and Ellicott City, Maryland, in May of 1830. Then on August 28, that short stretch of track would host a famous contest. The *Tom Thumb*, a tiny experimental steam engine, raced a horse belonging to the local stagecoach company.

Tom Thumb was designed and built by Peter Cooper, an inventor and manufacturer who had recently established an ironworks in Baltimore. He would later found the Cooper Union in New York City, which provides free instruction in art and science.

At first, the B&O's trains were hauled by horses, but the company had offered five hundred dollars to anyone who could produce a workable steam-powered alternative. Cooper took up the challenge and created his little vertical-boiler locomotive, powered by just a single cylinder. He provided a fan to create a greater draft for the fire.

With four men on the locomotive platform and thirty-six more (mostly directors of the B&O) in a boat-shaped car towed behind, the *Tom Thumb* chugged into motion, while the horse galloped along on a parallel track, hauling its own coach. *Tom Thumb* won on the outbound journey to Ellicott City. On the return, however, the fan belt snapped, which caused the fire to die and allowed the horse to pull ahead. The locomotive lost the race but won its point. Soon all Baltimore & Ohio trains were locomotive-hauled.

PETER COOPER'S "TOM THUMB" 1829-30 BALTIMORE & OHIO R.R.

Two

From Grasshoppers to Big Boys

WHAT WERE ENGINES CALLED, AND HOW do we categorize them?

The earliest locomotives often had descriptive names, like *Locomotion* or *Tom Thumb*. "Grasshoppers," a small group of locomotives with vertical boilers, had spindly beams that bobbed up and down — the motion that gave them their name.

In North America, the Whyte Classification System has been the most efficient way to categorize steam locomotives. It was created early in the twentieth century by Frederick Methvan Whyte, a mechanical engineer who worked for the New York Central. This numerical system counts the number of wheels on a locomotive in each category — lead truck, driving wheels, trailing truck. (A "truck" is a set of wheels with a common frame.) Thus a locomotive with a four-wheel lead truck, six driving wheels, and a four-wheel trailing truck is called a 4-6-4.

The small wheels of the lead truck support the weight of the cylinders and smokebox, both found at the front of the locomotive. They provide stability, leading the locomotive into curves. The much larger wheels in the center actually drive the locomotive, hence the name "driving wheels." The wheels of the trailing truck support the weight of the firebox and cab, at the rear of the locomotive.

◄ *This South African locomotive has a name (*Brenda*), type (*Mountain*), wheel arrangement (4-8-2), and class (19D). The train it pulls is the* Pride of Africa.

These Norfolk & Western locomotives — a 2-8-8-2 at left and a 2-6-6-4 — are much like the Union Pacific's famous 4-8-8-4 "Big Boy."

Names as Well as Numbers

The Whyte System is a useful method of classifying steam locomotives. Names are more interesting than numbers, however, and locomotives often had colorful names that told something about their histories.

Among the most common steam locomotives was the "Pacific," 4-6-2, first used on the Missouri Pacific. The "Northern," 4-8-4, was developed by the Northern Pacific. The "Mountain," 4-8-2, was first used in the mountainous territory of the coal-hauling Chesapeake & Ohio. The New

York Central also had 4-8-2s, but the railroad refused to call these locomotives "Mountains." Why? Because it advertised its New York City–Chicago main line as "The Water-Level Route — You Can Sleep," as opposed to the route of archrival Pennsylvania Railroad, which went through the Allegheny Mountains, with many grades and curves. So the New York Central called its 4-8-2s "Mohawks," after one of the rivers that made up the Water-Level Route.

The New York Central's most noted locomotives were its 4-6-4s, which it called "Hudsons" after yet another river on its route. This name was adopted by most railroads, as was "Berkshire" for a 2-8-4. These locomotives first ran through the Berkshire mountains of Massachusetts on the Boston & Albany, a subsidiary of the New York Central.

And then there was Union Pacific's "Big Boy," which was by most measures the largest locomotive ever built and hauled trains over Sherman Hill in Wyoming. This locomotive was a 4-8-8-4 (8-8 meaning it had two sets of driving wheels). It was built by the American Locomotive Company. Legend has it that when the locomotive was completed, a shopworker scrawled "Big Boy" in chalk on the locomotive's smokebox. The name stuck, though the Union Pacific might have preferred something more dignified.

Whatever formal names and classifications were given to locomotives, railroaders would refer to them in their own way. Sometimes they just used the locomotive's number, as in "Old 97."

Like many industries, steam railroading had a rich private language, words used by railroaders among themselves. Steam locomotives were often called "hogs," and the engineers who ran them "hogheads" or "hoggers." The men who shunted them back and forth in the engine terminal while they were being serviced were called "hostlers," a name originally applied to those who took care of horses at a stable or inn. The most widely used slang term for steam locomotive is "iron horse," which explains how "hostler" came to acquire its railroad meaning.

By whatever names or numbers, steam locomotives were a widely varied lot, changing hugely as they evolved over 130 years.

Chesapeake & Ohio's 4-8-4 No. 614 roars through a wintry day in West Virginia. A Southern railroad, the C & O chose the name "Greenbrier" rather than "Northern" for its 4-8-4s.

The Magic Word

"Pacific" was the magic word in the names of railroads themselves in the nineteenth and early twentieth centuries. It suggested grand plans to reach the distant western ocean. Both partners in the first transcontinental railroad, completed in 1869, claimed it: the Union Pacific and the Central Pacific, which later became part of the Southern Pacific. There were the Northern Pacific, the Western Pacific, and the Chicago, Milwaukee, St. Paul & Pacific. Railroads like the Chicago, Rock Island & Pacific and Duluth, Winnipeg & Pacific never got even close to the western ocean. The Butte, Anaconda & Pacific never built outside of Montana. Missouri Pacific was another of those roads that never reached its namesake ocean, but it did lend its name to one of the most famous locomotive types of all.

Above: This Pennsylvania Railroad locomotive was one of the most successful Pacifics ever built.

◄ *Left:* Nickel Plate Road 2-8-4 No. 759 —a Berkshire — blasts upgrade at Cresco, Pennsylvania, in the Pocono Mountains.

Right: This 2-6-2 Prairie totes empty sugar-cane cars ► at the Ifrain Alfonso mill in Cuba.

Three

Bigger and Better

THE "BIG BOY" AND OTHER GIANT LOCOMOTIVES of the mid-twentieth century were a far cry from the little "teakettles" that began the railroad age more than one hundred years earlier. As the decades rolled by, the most obvious change was, of course, size. Over time, passenger coaches and freight cars would grow bigger and heavier.

Thus locomotives had to grow heftier to do their job. Tracks became better, with taller, heavier rail. In the United States, where there was plenty of space, railroad rights-of-way, the land over which railroads are built, could be wide, allowing locomotives to grow big. In contrast, in densely settled Britain, where space was limited, locomotives had to be smaller. And it wasn't just size that made succeeding generations of steam locomotives faster and more powerful. Technology changed, too, and locomotives became more complex.

The evolution of the locomotive was also driven by a specific purpose. What kind of work was the engine to do? One obvious indicator of a locomotive's role has always been the size of its driving wheels: high for speed, low for power. Since freight trains have typically

◀ *Union Pacific's powerful Northern No. 8444 hauls an excursion in Wyoming. The big "elephant ears" at the front of the boiler are smoke deflectors, designed to keep the exhaust from blowing in the face of the engine crew.*

■ 23

This tank engine, which carries its own coal and water, runs on the Zig Zag Railway in Australia.

been heavier and longer than passenger trains, and speed more important in moving people than things, freight locomotives generally have low driving wheels and passenger locomotives high ones.

Tank engines were ideal for specific jobs. They carried their own fuel and water and didn't require a car called a tender coupled behind to carry these supplies. Tank engines had limited storage capacities. Unlike tender-equipped engines, they couldn't stray far from home. They were used primarily in short-distance service or for switching in yards. With no tender to get in the way, they had excellent visibility to the rear and could run in both directions — an advantage

in situations where it was impossible or too time-consuming to turn the locomotive at the end of its run.

A Variety of Gauges

Gauge is the distance between the rails. The standard gauge in the United States, Britain, and Europe is 4′ 8 1/2″. But track widths varied greatly in early railroading — and to a lesser extent still do today. Broad gauges, wider than standard, survive in Ireland, Spain and Portugal, Russia, India,

Australia, and elsewhere. Throughout much of Africa, the gauge norm is 3′ 6″— a size so typical of areas colonized by Britain that it is sometimes called "Imperial Gauge."

How did the odd width of 4′ 8 1/2″ come to be standard? Far-fetched as it may seem, it's because that was the width of Roman chariot and wagon wheels. In Britain, once part of the Roman Empire, the first railroads were wooden-railed, horse-drawn trams in the coal mines. The distance between rails, adopted there from wagons, spread to the steam railroads when they evolved later.

Why does gauge matter? Because the broader the gauge, the bigger and more powerful the locomotives can be, and thus the more they can haul. The narrower the gauge, the cheaper the railroad is to build, particularly in rugged country, where lots of tunnels and cuts through hills are required.

On the narrow-gauge Cumbres & Toltec Scenic Railroad, formerly part of the Denver & Rio Grande Western, a train rounds Tanglefoot Curve as it approaches Cumbres Pass in Colorado. This locomotive was called a "Mudhen" for its waddling gait.

The Great Locomotive Chase

The Civil War is considered the first conflict in which railroads played a major role. Certainly the railway superiority of the North helped the Union cause. Trains could move troops and supplies more quickly than any other transportation mode.

The Andrews Raid is the Civil War's most gripping railroad story, known as the "Great Locomotive Chase."

In April 1862, Union forces were marching on Chattanooga, Tennessee, and the Confederates were expected to move reinforcements there by rail from Atlanta. Hoping to prevent this, twenty Union soldiers in disguise, led by Major Andrews, had infiltrated Confederate territory.

At Big Shanty, Georgia, they hijacked the *General* while its crew and its passengers were having breakfast in the depot restaurant. Andrews's plan was to steam on to Chattanooga, burning bridges, tearing up rail, and cutting telegraph lines behind him.

But Fuller, the train's conductor, gave chase, first on a handcar and then in a small industrial locomotive. Though the Andrews party had a good head start and could travel faster, they were delayed waiting for oncoming trains on the single-track line. At Kingston, Georgia, they were stopped for more than an hour. When they steamed off, Fuller and his posse were just minutes behind. He commandeered the *Texas* and continued the chase.

Andrews never did get far enough ahead to perform the intended sabotage. Finally, after a nail-biting eight hours and eighty-seven miles, the *General* ran out of fuel. As its fire died, it rolled to a stop. Andrews and his men scattered, but all were captured — and the seven highest-ranking soldiers were shot.

The Evolution of Steam Locomotives

Locomotive designers were always seeking a better way of doing things. The first change was the addition of the "lead truck" to a locomotive with just driving wheels, helping the locomotive track through curves. Thus developed the 4-4-0 or "American Standard," which indeed was the standard locomotive for many decades. The Civil War's famous "Great Locomotive Chase" from Big Shanty, Georgia, involved two American Standards, the *General* and the *Texas*. Two more American Standards, the Central Pacific's *Jupiter* and Union Pacific's No. 119, met at Promontory, Utah, in 1869 for the driving of the Golden Spike. This ceremony, which marked the completion of the first transcontinental railroad, was among the great moments in American history.

In time the more powerful 4-6-0s, or "Ten-wheelers," and 2-8-0s, or "Consolidations," would take over from the American Standards. Next came the addition of the "trailing truck" under the firebox and locomotive cab, which allowed engines to grow still bigger and heavier.

The final influence in the way steam locomotives looked arrived in the 1930s, in the midst of the Great Depression, with the passion for streamlining. Industrial designers were imposing a sleek, streamlined look to every-thing from buildings to vacuum cleaners and refrigerators. In railroading, this style was first and most successfully applied to diesel locomotives, just then appearing on the scene. In order to keep pace with this innovation, some railroads covered up their angular steam locomotives with smooth metal shrouding, making them better matches for the new stream-lined passenger trains.

Among the last streamlined steamers to see regular

American Standard 119 is typical of the locomotive type that dominated railroading in the United States in the latter decades of the nineteenth century. Number 119 is a replica of the Union Pacific locomotive that was present for the driving of the Golden Spike. Here, it steams at the National Historic Site at Promontory, Utah, where this great event is routinely reenacted.

Canadian Pacific's once-proud streamlined "Royal Hudsons" by 1959 had been reduced to hauling commuters to and from Montreal. All locomotives in the class originally wore crowns on their running boards.

service in the United States were Norfolk & Western's powerful J-class 4-8-4s. The last in Canada were Canadian Pacific's elegant "Royal Hudsons." These locomotives acquired their name in 1939 when one of them hauled the Royal Train carrying King George VI and Queen Elizabeth westward across Canada.

Somehow, though, streamlining never seemed entirely right on a steam locomotive. Its beauty was in the way its shape and machinery showed what it did and how.

Right: *The crew members look oversized in the cab of these small locomotives on the* ▶
2-foot 6-inch– gauge Esquel Branch of Argentina's General Roca Railroad.

Four

How a Steam Locomotive Works

THE BASIC IDEA IS SIMPLE: The heat of fire turns water to steam. When the steam expands — and it does, hugely — it pushes a piston, which moves a driving rod, which turns a wheel, which is linked to the other driving wheels by connecting rods. Thus the locomotive moves — and pulls many, many times its own weight.

The key to it all is that water, when it turns to steam in the atmosphere, expands in volume sixteen hundred times. Building on this scientific phenomenon, locomotive designers over the years created machines capable of producing great power and speed.

One such machine is No. 700, a 4-8-4 built in 1938 by the Baldwin Locomotive Company for the Spokane, Portland & Seattle, a small railroad in the Northwest. By a happy chain of circumstances, this engine, an oil-burner, can occasionally be seen in operation today. When the SP&S switched to diesel locomotives in 1954, the railroad gave No. 700 to the city of Portland, Oregon, for display in a park. Thirty years later, a group of volunteers, who called themselves the Pacific Railroad Preservation Association, began restoring No. 700 to operating condition.

The cutaway drawing of No. 700 (p. 33) shows how a modern steam locomotive works. Inside the firebox, the fuel — typically coal, but in the case of the SP&S locomotive, oil — is ignited. The

◄ *In Montana, Spokane, Portland & Seattle No. 700 struts its stuff for its fans on a chilly October morning. Steam condensing in the cold air creates the white "smoke."*

The "backhead" of a South African Beyer-Garratt locomotive shows an array of gauges and controls.

firetube boiler, nearly filled with water, surrounds the firebox. The firetubes, or flues, open into the firebox and extend through the boiler to the smokebox at the front of the locomotive. Hot gases from the firebox pass through the flues, heating the water in the boiler and creating steam, which is captured in the steam dome atop the boiler. (Most locomotives have a second dome. It holds sand, which can be piped down to the tracks to provide traction for the driving wheels when the rails are slippery.)

From the steam dome, steam flows to the cylinders when the engineer opens the throttle. On modern locomotives like the 700, this steam passes on the way through superheater pipes within the flues, raising its temperature dramatically and making it fifty percent more powerful. An all-important feature of the steam dome is the safety or "pop" valve, which releases when the steam pressure reaches a certain point (260 pounds per square inch for SP&S 700). "Popping off" is what prevents boiler explosions.

The smokebox of SP&S 700 has a well-proportioned elegance with numberboards (reading "700"), bell, and headlight. The white metal flags and lights (called "markers") indicate that the train is "running extra," meaning that it is unscheduled.

The Sound of Steam

Steam enters the cylinder alternately on either side of the piston, moving it back and forth. (A complex assemblage of rods and hangers called the "valve gear" opens and closes the cylinder valves.) The driving rods link the piston to the driving wheels, and the connecting or side rods link the wheels to each other. The exhaust steam passes from the cylinders through the smokebox and out the smokestack. The partial vacuum created in the smokebox sucks the hot air and gases through the flues, creating a draft that fans the flames in the firebox. A mixture of firebox smoke and exhaust steam goes up the stack in a rhythm matching the movement of the pistons. This is what creates the chugging sound so characteristic of the steam locomotive.

Stand in the cab of a modern steam locomotive and you'll see a dizzying array of valves, gauges, handles, and levers. There is, of course, the throttle, and the reversing wheel or lever, which in function is roughly equivalent to the gearshift on an automobile. There's a water glass, which shows the water level in the boiler, and a gauge showing the boiler pressure. There are gauges reading the air-brake pressure, and two brake handles — one for the engine's brakes and one for the train's. There's the injector, which forces water into the boiler. And all this is just the beginning.

A steam locomotive is truly a wonderful collection of moving parts, most of them right out in plain view. Rarely has there ever been a machine so alive.

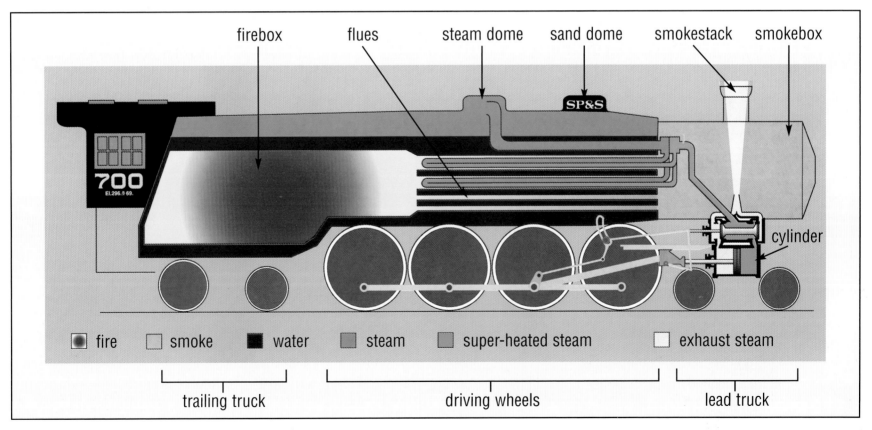

This cutaway diagram shows the working parts of Spokane, Portland & Seattle No. 700.

Five

The Care and Feeding of the Iron Horses

IRON HORSES REQUIRED AS MUCH ATTENTION as real horses — maybe more. They needed to be fed frequently. They needed to be groomed. They needed a practiced, careful touch on their "reins," or throttle. Often they needed doctoring.

A steam locomotive was a high-maintenance machine. And the labor needed to run it was intensive. That was part of its charm. But it was an even greater part of its demise. All this attention was expensive, especially as the years went by and labor costs increased. This was perhaps the major factor that doomed steam, eventually sending steam locomotives to the scrap line or, in a few happy cases, to museums.

Steam locomotives had a voracious appetite for fuel and water, and they craved other attention. Their many moving parts needed to be oiled and greased.

Locomotives needed their fireboxes cleaned, unless they were oil-burners. The earliest locomotive fuel was wood, which remained the norm for decades, until it was replaced by coal. Coal ruled from then on, except on the few railroads, mainly in the West, that switched

◀ In Montreal's St. Luc Yard, a Pacific takes on coal.

A Guayaquil & Quito 2-8-0 takes water in Huigra, Ecuador.

Cleaning the fires at the engine terminal at Chama, New Mexico, on the Cumbres & Toltec Scenic Railroad.

to oil because of its greater availability in their region and the reduced fire danger it represented.

Where wood or coal was burned in the firebox, the exhausted fuel — ashes and "clinkers" — had to be raked out every so often if the fire were to burn hot. The fireman could do this from the locomotive cab by shaking the firebox grates and thrusting a long-handled rake through the firebox door. But before and after every run, in the engine terminal, the firebox was thoroughly cleaned and the ashes dropped into a pit.

Railroads Organized Around the Locomotive's Needs

It was the steam locomotive's need for attention that shaped the way railroads were structured. In the early years, a locomotive's range was about one hundred miles, so railroads were split into "divisions" of roughly that length. At "division points," major towns grew up — "railroad towns" that thrived on the employment offered by the railroad. Locomotive and train crews were changed there. Freight trains would be switched, their cars sorted for different destinations. All this required manpower.

Typically, there'd be a roundhouse, with tracks spoking off a turntable (a revolving bridge used to get a locomotive headed in the right direction for its next assignment). In the roundhouse, locomotives were stored between runs. They'd be lubricated and perhaps wiped down to remove road grime from their boilers. "Running repairs" — light maintenance — would be performed there.

At one location along the railroad would be the "back shops," the site of heavy repairs and rebuilding. Here even more workers would be employed in a wide variety of crafts

A Canadian Pacific Ten-wheeler approaches the octagonal water tank at Campbell's Bay, Quebec.

that ranged from welder to boilermaker. Some railroads even built their own locomotives, giving rise to the greatest railroad towns of all: Altoona, Pennsylvania, on the Pennsylvania Railroad, for instance, and Roanoke, Virginia, on the Norfolk & Western.

But fuel and water were the steam locomotive's most constant need, and the structures erected to meet it were among the most memorable parts of the railroad scene. Water supplies were strategically placed all along the railroad so engines could stop along the way for refreshment. Water might flow directly from a tank through a spout or be delivered from a remote tank by a trackside "water plug," a tall, freestanding spout that could be swung over the tender.

Getting Coal to the Firebox

"Coaling up" usually took place at the terminals. But sometimes towers containing coal were erected on the main lines so locomotives could be fed along the way. Wherever they were, these towers were eye-catching, often soaring structures, highlights of any skyline.

Of course, the coal had to be moved from the tender into the firebox, and for many years that was accomplished only by the strong arms and back of the fireman, using his shovel (or "scoop," as it was generally known in a locomotive cab) and skill. It was hard, dirty work, but building and maintaining a good fire required brains as well as brawn. Different locomotives — even two seemingly identical ones of the same class — might require different firing techniques. The fireman had to know how to build different fires, light or heavy, depending on the terrain. If the locomotive needed to climb a mountain, a heavy fire would be required. It took a skilled fireman to get a locomotive over the road successfully.

A fireman cracks the "butterfly" doors to check his handiwork.

Earl Knoob adjusts the air brake on a Cumbres & Toltec 2-8-2.

Bucket and scoop in South Africa.

But of all steam-era railroaders, the most exalted was the engineer, the envy of generations of young boys (and no doubt of some young girls — a number of today's diesel-locomotive engineers are women). While it was the fireman who fed the locomotive, it was the engineer who babied it, who coaxed it into performing its best. Like the rider on a horse who knows his mount's moods and capabilities, the locomotive engineer, his gloved hand on the throttle, was connected by special bond with his machine. He knew just when to push, and when to ease off. He knew every mile of railroad, in every kind of weather, with every size and type of train connected to his locomotive's tail.

And he knew what to do with the whistle cord. With a deft touch, he could make the whistle shout with urgency or moan with melancholy, announcing in a very personal way his comings and goings.

On the Black River & Western in New Jersey, Elizabeth Griswold and Kevin Knobl wipe down 2-8-0 No. 60.

Casey Jones, Brave Engineer

"Come all you rounders if you want to hear
A story about a brave engineer.
Casey Jones was the rounder's name,
On a six eight-wheeler, boys, he won his fame."

On April 29, 1900, with Casey Jones at the throttle and Sim Webb in the fireman's seat of Engine 382, Illinois Central Railroad's train No. 1 left Memphis, Tennessee, for Canton, Mississippi, more than an hour off schedule.

Later, running fast to make up time, Casey and his six-car passenger train approached a passing siding at Vaughan, Mississippi. There, a freight train was stalled, partially on the main line. A flagman had been sent out to signal ongoing trains to stop.

Casey didn't see him — or the stalled freight, until it was too late. Then he put the brakes into emergency, turned on the sander, and threw the locomotive into reverse.

"Jump, Sim!" he shouted to his fireman, and Sim did. But Casey stayed aboard, like a captain going down with his ship. He was the only one killed when No. 382 crashed into the freight.

Wallace Sanders, an engine wiper at Canton and friend of Casey's, wrote a ballad about the wreck. The song spread up and down the Illinois Central. Some vaudeville performers heard it and put it in their act, assuring that Casey Jones would be the most famous engineer ever.

Six

Steam Bows Out

IN TIME, THE STEAM LOCOMOTIVE whistle's soaring cry was no longer heard across the land.

After hauling trains for more than a century, steam finally met its match in the more efficient diesel locomotives. One by one those dramatic, eye-catching steam machines were shunted off onto scrap lines. With no more fire in their bellies, they were like living things that had died. Eventually almost all the hundreds of thousands of steam locomotives that had hauled the world's trains were cut up for scrap.

What caused their demise? Developing technology, such as "internal combustion," where the fuel is burned within the cylinder, as in gasoline or diesel engines. That's how the automobile works. The diesel locomotive is far more fuel-efficient than a steamer, and almost as easy to maintain as a car. No longer were boilermakers or machinists or welders needed. Coaling towers and water tanks could be torn down.

The locomotive that most significantly began the revolution that would doom steam was FT No. 103, built by the Electro-Motive Division of General Motors. In 1940 this locomotive (actually four locomotives coupled together) toured the country, trying to sell itself to the various railroads.

◄ *Burlington Northern Santa Fe diesel locomotives at Lombard, Montana.*

Diesels Finally Win

Though the advantages of the FT were clear, the railroad industry was slow to change. Managers had watched steam locomotives hauling trains all their lives — and knew others had been doing so for many generations before their own. Though the Santa Fe ordered some FTs, and many other railroads eventually followed, it took another two decades for the diesel to completely vanquish the steam locomotive.

When railroaders speak of "diesel" locomotives, they technically mean diesel-electric. Aboard these locomotives, a diesel-powered generator provides electricity, which in turn drives traction motors that actually power the locomotive. Straight electric locomotives are something else again. Never used extensively in the United States — today their territory is essentially limited to Amtrak's "Northeast Corridor," from Washington to Boston — electrics are common throughout most of Europe.

These electric locomotives have their own drama, speeding silently across the countryside. But next to a breathing, steaming iron horse, alive even when at rest, the electrics and diesels seem tame and static.

In 1983, one of the Pennsylvania Railroad's graceful and powerful GG1 electrics is celebrated at the end of a career that spanned nearly half a century.

Seen on the Milwaukee Road near Ontonagon, Michigan, this quartet of diesels is a slightly younger cousin of the FTs that revolutionized railroading.

Seven

All Aboard for a Ride Behind Steam

WHEN THE AGE OF STEAM ENDED on North American railroads, a fascinating, flamboyant chapter closed. Happily, though, a few steam locomotives did escape the scrapper's torch. They were placed in parks, as monuments to the golden age of railroading. They became part of museum collections. Best of all, some were put to work hauling tourists and train fans on short excursions, so even today we can appreciate the timeless attraction of the steam locomotive at work.

In all, fewer than two thousand steam locomotives survive in North America, many of them sadly deteriorated through years of neglect and exposure to the elements. Of these, some 150 currently operate.

Elsewhere around the world, the same changeover from steam to diesel and electric occurred, generally later than in the United States and Canada. And other countries have saved some locomotives, too, with Great Britain being the leader in railway preservation. On many dozens of little railroads, then, on summer weekends particularly, steam locomotives spring to life again, ready to haul their passengers back in time.

◄ *On Pennsylvania's narrow-gauge East Broad Top Railroad, 2-8-2s climb upgrade to McMullen's Summit.*

In Pennsylvania, the East Broad Top, once an iron- and later a coal-hauler, offers visitors an almost perfectly preserved slice of 1920s railroading: steam engines, passenger coaches, freight cars, roundhouse, turntable, depot and general offices, and shop buildings.

In Colorado and New Mexico, two pieces of the vast Denver & Rio Grande Western system survive — the Durango & Silverton Narrow Gauge Railroad and Cumbres & Toltec Scenic Railroad. Both railroads offer breathtakingly beautiful rides behind steam through western landscapes — and a good understanding of the region's railroad history.

Britain has more than one hundred preserved lines, and other countries have outstanding lines as well. In South Africa, a branch of the nationalized transportation system maintains a fleet of historic locomotives, operating them on a train called the *Union Limited*. Rohan Vos, a wealthy South African, operates the *Pride of Africa*, a luxury passenger excursion that leaves its home base of Pretoria behind steam.

Steam on the Main Line

Aboard the *Union Limited* and *Pride of Africa*, passengers ride at speed on the main line behind steam — an experience rare today in the United States. Though Union Pacific operates its 4-8-4 and 4-6-6-4 — called a "Challenger," a slightly smaller brother to the Big Boy — a few times each year, main-line steam excursions are scarce. Tracks have become more and more congested with freight trains, and insurance costs have soared.

But the chance to stand at trackside and watch a big, modern steam locomotive roar by does still exist. Imagine, for instance, that you're somewhere in Montana, and the SP&S 700 is approaching at full tilt, gray smoke boiling from the stack. The whistle screams a warning as the locomotive storms through a road crossing, where automobiles humbly wait. With sun glinting from its shiny boiler, driving rods flailing wildly, and blue-clad engineer waving in a friendly way, the noble locomotive flashes by, shaking the ground, and tears off toward the horizon with its long train. A few minutes later, only the distant moan of whistle and a dark smudge of smoke against the sky recall its passage.

A Grand Canyon Railway train winds through Coconino Canyon in Arizona.

Author's Note

Now that you've read about steam locomotives, why not go out and see one that's alive and running? Better yet, climb aboard and ride.

Scattered across the United States are numerous rail museums, and steam-powered railroads that are run for tourists and enthusiasts. The best single source of information about these organizations is *Tourist Trains*, which lists railroad museums, displays, preservations, and historic operations, whether steam, diesel, or electric. It can be purchased at most rail museums and tourist railroads.

Listed below are some places around the country where you can see steam locomotives in operation. All are to some extent seasonal, and some run only on weekends. Others use diesel locomotives at times of lesser demand. Be sure to check ahead before planning a trip.

California State Railroad Museum, Sacramento, California. (916) 445-6645, *http://www.csrmf.org*.

Cass Scenic Railroad, Cass, West Virginia. (800) 225-5982, *http://www.cassrailroad.com*.

Cumbres & Toltec Scenic Railroad, Chama, New Mexico. (888) 286-2737, *http://www.cumbrestoltec.com*.

Durango & Silverton Narrow-Gauge Railroad, Durango, Colorado. (888) 872-4607, *http://www.durangotrain.com*.

East Broad Top Railroad, Rockhill Furnace, Pennsylvania. (814) 447-3011, *http://www.ebtrr.com*.

Grand Canyon Railway, Williams, Arizona. (800) 843-8724, *http://www.thetrain.com*.

Illinois Railway Museum, Union, Illinois. (800) 244-7245, *http://www.irm.org*.

Mount Washington Cog Railway, Mount Washington, New Hampshire. (800) 922-8825, *http://www.thecog.com*.

Nevada Northern Railway, East Ely, Nevada. (866) 407-8326, *http://www.nevadanorthernrailway.net*.

Strasburg Rail Road, Strasburg, Pennsylvania. (717) 687-7522, *http://www.strasburgrailroad.com*.

Steamtown National Historic Site, Scranton, Pennsylvania. (888) 693-9391, *http://www.nps.gov/stea/index.htm*.

Valley Railroad, Essex, Connecticut. (860) 767-0103, *http://www.valleyrr.com*.

Western Maryland Scenic Railroad, Cumberland, Maryland. (800) 872-4650, *http://www.wmsr.com*.

Happy riding! —Karl Zimmermann

Glossary

Boiler: The largest component of a steam locomotive, with flues running through it. The boiler holds the water as it's converted to steam.

Cab: On a steam engine the space, almost always behind the boiler, where the engineer and fireman work and control the locomotive.

Depot: A modest, usually small-town railroad station.

Driving rod: Links the piston with the large wheels that power a steam locomotive.

Driving wheels: Joined to one another by a connecting rod, these large wheels move the locomotive along the rails.

Engineer: Called a "driver" in Great Britain, he controls the locomotive.

Firebox: Area at the rear of the boiler with grates for a coal fire or jets for an oil fire. Here the hot gases are generated that pass through the flues to heat the water in the boiler.

Fireman: Second person in a locomotive cab whose task on a steam locomotive is to tend the fire. Firemen worked aboard diesels for many years, essentially as assistant engineers, though their job has now been eliminated.

Gauge: The distance between a track's two rails, measured from the inside edges.

Lead truck: Wheels at the front of a locomotive that carry the weight of the smokebox and help "lead" the locomotive around curves.

Piston: A piece that slides back and forth inside a locomotive's cylinder as steam is admitted, first to one side and then the other. This movement is what powers the engine.

Pullman: A sleeping car, named for George M. Pullman, whose company would come to build, own, and operate virtually all the sleepers in the United States.

Roundhouse: A circular building (shaped that way to accommodate tracks spoking off a turntable) where locomotives are stored and serviced. In the biggest rail centers, roundhouses were full circles. Typically, though, they would be smaller—just an arc.

Smokebox: The round space at the front of a locomotive, ahead of the boiler, where the smoke and hot gases that have passed through the flues gather before being exhausted through the smokestack.

Steam dome: The hump on the top of a locomotive boiler where steam gathers before being directed to the cylinders.

Tender: Car coupled directly behind a steam locomotive to carry water and fuel (most often coal).

Trailing truck: Wheels below the locomotive cab that carry the weight of the firebox.

Index

Africa, 9, 25, 46
American Standard, 26
Australia, 25

Baltimore & Ohio Railroad, 14, 15
Berkshire, 18
Best Friend of Charleston, 14
Big Boy, 19, 23, 46
Boston & Albany Railroad, 19
Britain, 13, 23, 25, 45, 46

Camden & Amboy Railroad, 15
Canada, 9, 28, 45
Canadian Pacific, 9, 28
Central Pacific, 26
Challenger, 46
Chesapeake & Ohio, 18
Civil War, 26
Classifications, 17–19
coal, 6, 7, 13, 35, 38
Cooper, Peter, 15
crew, 38–39
Cumbres & Toltec Scenic Railroad, 46

Delaware & Hudson Canal Company, 13
demise, 6, 7, 9, 35, 41–42, 45
Denver & Rio Grande Western, 46
diesels, 6, 26, 31, 41–42, 45
Durango & Silverton Narrow Gauge Railroad, 46

East Broad Top, 46
electrics, 42, 45
engineers, 39, 46
Europe, 9, 24, 42. *See also* Britain

firemen (railroad crewmen), 38
FT No. 103, 41

gauge, 24–25
General, 26
Great Locomotive Chase, 26
Golden Spike, 26
Grasshoppers, 17

hazards, 14. *See also* Jones, Casey
vs. horses, 15
Hudson, 18

Illinois Central, 39

Jones, Casey, 39
John Bull, 15
Jupiter, 26

lingo, railroader, 19
Liverpool & Manchester Railway, 13
Locomotion, 17

maintenance, 35–39
manufacturers, 13–15, 19, 26, 31; diesel, 41–42
Missouri Pacific, 18
Mohawk, 18
Mountain, 18

New York Central, 17–19
No. 700, 31, 32, 33, 46
Norfolk & Western Railway, 6, 28, 37
Northern, 18
Northern Pacific, 18

oil, as fuel, 36
operation, 11, 15, 17, 26, 31–33; illustrated, 33
origins, 11–15

Pacific, 18, 20
Pennsylvania Railroad, 6, 15, 18, 37
Pride of Africa, 46

rails. *See* track
Rocket, 13
roundhouses, 36
Royal Hudsons, 28

safety, 14–15, 32. *See also* hazards
South America, 9
South Carolina Railroad, 14
Spokane, Portland & Seatle, 31, 46
steam, 11, 31
Stephenson, George, 13, 15
Stockton & Darlington, 13
Stourbridge Lion, 13–14
streamlining, 26–28

Texas (locomotive), 26
Tom Thumb, 14–15, 17
tourism, 9, 31, 45–46
towns, railroad, 36, 37
track, 24. *See also* gauge
trucks (locomotive components), 17, 26

Union Limited, 46
Union Pacific, 19, 26, 46

water, 37. *See also* steam
wheels. *See* trucks
Whyte, Frederick Methvan, 17
Whyte Classification System, 17–18
women, as engineers, 39

THE "STOURBRIDGE LION,"
THE FIRST LOCOMOTIVE EVER RUN UPON A RAILROAD IN AMERICA.

Copyright, 1883, by John Torrey.